Baby animals in wetland habitats

Bobbie Kalman

Crabtree Publishing Company

www.crabtreebooks.com

The Habitats of Baby Animals

Created by Bobbie Kalman

Dedicated by Katherine Berti—to Ken, Winnie, and your precious new baby boy, David Miura.

"Ten tiny little fingers that always want to play, that never stop exploring the wonder of today. Ten tiny little fingers that from the very start, will reach out for tomorrow yet always hold your heart."

Author and Editor-in-Chief
Bobbie Kalman

Editors
Kathy Middleton
Crystal Sikkens

Design
Bobbie Kalman
Katherine Berti
Samantha Crabtree
(front cover)

Photo research
Bobbie Kalman

Print and production coordinator
Katherine Berti

Prepress technician
Katherin Berti

Illustrations
Bonna Rouse: page 22

Photographs
BigStockPhoto: page 17 (top)
Lauren Kinsey/sweetmagnoliaphoto.com:
    pages 17 (bottom right), 24 (bottom left)
Photos.com: page 11 (alligator hatchling)
Jim Scarff: front cover, page 15 (top)
Other photographs by Shutterstock

Library and Archives Canada Cataloguing in Publication

Kalman, Bobbie, 1947-
    Baby animals in wetland habitats / Bobbie Kalman.

(The habitats of baby animals)
Includes index.
Issued also in electronic format.
ISBN 978-0-7787-7730-4 (bound).--ISBN 978-0-7787-7743-4 (pbk.)

    1. Wetland animals--Infancy--Juvenile literature. 2. Wetland ecology--Juvenile literature. I. Title. II. Series: Kalman, Bobbie, 1947- . Habitats of baby animals.

QL113.8.K34 2011   j591.3'9091   C2010-907489-0

Library of Congress Cataloging-in-Publication Data

Kalman, Bobbie.
  Baby animals in wetland habitats / Bobbie Kalman.
      p. cm. -- (The habitats of baby animals)
  Includes index.
  ISBN 978-0-7787-7743-4 (pbk. : alk. paper) -- ISBN 978-0-7787-7730-4 (reinforced library binding : alk. paper) -- ISBN 978-1-4271-9605-7 (electronic (pdf))
  1. Wetland animals--Infancy--Juvenile literature. 2. Wetland animals--Ecology--Juvenile literature. I. Title.
  QL113.8.K35 2011
  591.768--dc22

                                                   2010047657

Crabtree Publishing Company

www.crabtreebooks.com   1-800-387-7650

Printed in China/022011/RG20101116

Published in Canada
Crabtree Publishing
616 Welland Ave.
St. Catharines, Ontario
L2M 5V6

Published in the United States
Crabtree Publishing
PMB 59051
350 Fifth Avenue, 59th Floor
New York, New York 10118

Published in the United Kingdom
Crabtree Publishing
Maritime House
Basin Road North, Hove
BN41 1WR

Published in Australia
Crabtree Publishing
386 Mt. Alexander Rd.
Ascot Vale (Melbourne)
VIC 3032

What is in this book?

What is a habitat?

A **habitat** is a place in nature. Plants and animals live in habitats. They are **living things**. Living things grow, change, and make new living things. Plants make new plants, and animals make babies, like this baby alligator.

What is a wetland?

A **wetland** is a kind of habitat. It is land that is covered with water. Some wetlands are covered with water all year. Other wetlands are covered with water for only part of the year. Wetlands provide animals with places to live and to raise their young.

Living and non-living

Habitats are made up of living and **non-living things**. Air, sunshine, rocks, soil, and water are non-living things. Living things need non-living things. They also need other living things, such as plants and animals. Living things find the things they need in their habitats, such as water to drink, food to eat, and shelter.

Water is a very important part of wetland habitats. The living things in wetlands live in or close to water. This mother moorhen is making a nest for her baby chicks.

Many kinds of **wading** birds can be seen in wetlands. Wading birds are birds with long legs that **wade**, or walk slowly through water, to find food. These roseate spoonbills sweep their long beaks through water to catch frogs, newts, bugs, and small fish.

Two kinds of wetlands

There are two main kinds of wetlands. They are **swamps** and **marshes**. Swamps are wetlands with trees. They are covered with water for part of the year. Many swamps have **fresh water**. Fresh water does not have a lot of salt in it. Swamps that are close to oceans have **salt water**, which contains a lot of salt.

This alligator lives in a swamp.

What are marshes?

Marshes are shallow, grassy wetlands without trees. They are covered with water all year. Marshes are along the edges of lakes, rivers, and ponds. Many kinds of animals live in or near marshes.

This raccoon finds food in a marsh.

Wetland babies

Some of the animals that live in
wetlands are rabbits, cougars,
raccoons, opossums, turtles,
alligators, crocodiles, ducks,
and many kinds of birds.
What are the names of
these baby animals?

*turtle
hatchling*

*cougar
cub*

bunny rabbit

opossum joey

raccoon kits

duckling

alligator hatchling

crocodile hatchling

11

Baby reptiles hatch

Alligators and crocodiles are **reptiles** that live most of their adult lives in water. When it is time for the reptile mothers to lay eggs, they leave their water habitats to lay their eggs on land. An alligator or crocodile mother builds a nest of grass and mud and lays her eggs inside. She covers the nest with plants and guards it until the eggs hatch.

Before hatching, the babies let out loud noises to let their mother know that they are ready to hatch. The mother then digs out the eggs.

Each baby breaks its egg using an egg tooth.

The mothers carry their babies back to the water and look after them for up to two years. This alligator mother is carrying her babies on her back.

*The hatchlings stay close in groups called **pods**.*

Birds and chicks

Many kinds of birds live in wetland habitats. Wetlands are also very important places for birds that **migrate**. Migrating birds fly to warmer places for winter and stop at wetlands for food and water. Many bird mothers in wetlands take care of their babies until the chicks can take care of themselves.

Like alligators, baby birds also hatch from eggs. This great white egret has built a nest for her eggs and chicks. The chicks will stay in the nest until they can fly.

Many bird fathers also help take care of their chicks. This father is bringing up food from his stomach into a chick's mouth. Some baby birds are fed this way.

Mother ducks teach their ducklings how to swim. Some ducklings are afraid to go into the water. Two of these ducklings are riding on their mother's back. They are not quite ready to swim yet.

Mammal babies

Mammals are animals with hair or fur. Mammal babies do not hatch from eggs. They are born live. After their babies are born, mammal mothers feed them milk from their bodies. Drinking mother's milk is called **nursing**. The opossum below nurses many babies. Most mammal mothers look after their young. They keep their babies safe and teach them how to hunt or find food.

*An opossum is a mammal called a **marsupial**. A marsupial mother has a fur-lined pouch where her joeys nurse and grow. These joeys are too big for the pouch, so their mother is carrying them on her back.*

Rabbit mothers keep their babies safe in **burrows**, or holes, under the ground.

The Florida panther is a type of cougar. It lives in the swamps of southern Florida. There are not many of these animals left. Panther cubs have spots and blue eyes.

Cold bodies

Some wetland animals spend most of their time in the water. Frogs, turtles, alligators, and crocodiles come out of the water to **bask**, or sunbathe. They are **cold-blooded** animals. Cold-blooded animals need to warm their bodies in the sun. They cannot heat their bodies from the inside the way **warm-blooded** animals can.

These adult and baby turtles are basking on a rock in the water.

This baby alligator has found a sunny spot for basking among some plants.

This young frog is basking on a lily pad. Part of its body is keeping cool in water.

Wetland food

There is plenty of food to eat in wetlands. Some wetland animals eat mainly plants. Animals that eat plants are called **herbivores**. Rabbits are herbivores. They eat grasses, flowers, and weeds. Most wading birds are **carnivores**, or animals that eat other animals. Wading birds eat fish, clams, frogs, and small reptiles.

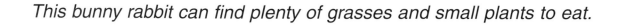

This bunny rabbit can find plenty of grasses and small plants to eat.

This young heron has caught a catfish to eat in its wetland habitat.

Wetland food chain

Animals need **energy**, or power. They need energy to breathe, move, grow, and stay alive. They get their energy from eating other living things. Plants do not eat other things. They make their own food from sunlight, air, and water. Making food from sunlight is called **photosynthesis**.

Leaves take in sunlight.

Leaves take in air.

long stems

A plant gets sunlight through its leaves. It also gets air through its leaves. A plant gets water through its roots. Many wetland plants have long stems so their leaves can catch sunlight above water.

The roots are in the soil.

22

sun

A wetland food chain

A **food chain** is the passing of energy from one living thing to another. When an animal eats another animal that has eaten a plant, there is a food chain. The food chain on this page is in a marsh. It is made up of plants, a rabbit, and a cougar.

Plants make food. They contain the sun's energy.

When the bunny eats the plants, it gets some of the sun's energy from the plants.

When the cougar eats the bunny, some of the energy that was in the plants and the bunny is passed along to the cougar.

23

Words to know and Index

alligators
pages 4, 8, 10, 11, 12–13, 18, 19

babies
pages 4, 6, 10–11, 12–13, 14–15, 16–17, 18, 19

birds
pages 6, 7, 14–15, 20

crocodiles
pages 10, 11, 12, 18, 19

food
pages 6, 7, 9, 14, 15, 16, 20–21, 22–23

food chain
pages 22–23

Other index words
carnivores page 20
cold-blooded
pages 18–19
habitats pages 4–5, 6, 12, 14, 21
herbivores page 20
living things pages 4, 6, 22, 23
mammals pages 16–17
non-living things page 6
nursing page 16
photosynthesis page 22
plants pages 4, 12, 19, 20, 22, 23
reptiles pages 12–13

mothers
pages 6, 12, 13, 14, 15, 16, 17

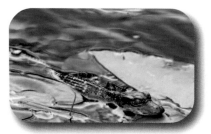

wetlands
pages 5, 6, 7, 8–9, 14, 18, 20, 21, 23